The Business of Ministry

Part 1

Annilia Wright-Mosley

Project Manager: Annilia Wright-Mosley
Cover Design: Elroy Forbes
Executive Editor: Holly Layman
Forward: Dr. Michael L. Mosley

ISBN-13: 978-1542984720
ISBN-10:1542984726

Table of Contents

Part 1

Foreword

God spoke to Moses and asked him a thought-provoking question, "What is that you have in your hands?" When faced with the seemingly impossible situation of the Red Sea in front of him, and the tormenting taunts of the past, Pharaoh's army, behind him, Moses needed divine instruction.

In your hands right now are divine instructions that will help to manifest the gifts, ideas, and inspirations of your heart. You may be a preacher, lyricist, author, singer, or musical composer ready to spread your talent with the world. It has been stated for centuries, "Knowledge is power." Now you have the opportunity to use the knowledge you're holding in your hands to become "powerful."

Glean from the knowledge of this leading music business leader, whom many have described as being motivating and encouraging, but beyond it all, as her husband, I can say she is certainly sincere. My darling Annilia will encourage you to maintain your spiritual gifting while adding some professional insight for creating a productive "Business of Ministry!"

Dr. Michael L. Mosley
Prophet/ Pastor
Intuitive Life Coach

Acknowledgements

I want to thank God, my creator and guide on earth, for giving me a passion to serve others. I also want to thank my parents, Douglas Wright, Sr. and Rosalind Wright, for loving and supporting me in every phase of my life, and for instilling in me the importance of being a worshipper of God, giver to those less fortunate than I, a forgiver of those who misused me, a lover of family; of being loyal to righteousness, and a peacemaker to humanity. I also want to thank one of my Sheroes, Mary Lousie Cooper (my grandma), for being an example of strength and wisdom. If it weren't for you, I would never have pursued a career in the music industry. I thank you for your act of faith, for being the vessel and investor starting my sister and me in the gospel music industry.

I want to thank my faithful godparents who have also been in my life to give me great counsel and support in my ministry initiatives over the years. I thank the spiritual fathers and mothers whom I've had the honor to serve with throughout my ministry career.

To every BOSS I had the honor of working and serving with, I thank you for contributing to my business development in life.

I want to thank every family

member who has pushed me over the years and supported my efforts to bring value to others' lives and my community.

Thank you to every investor who has believed in my visions and contributed to my success over the years.

I want to thank and acknowledge Telisa Stinson, Jerry Mannery, the late James Moore, Rochelle Brown, Sam Williams, D.A. Johnson, Andre Montel, Billy Daniels, Bro Steve, Monica Butler, Richard Manson, Dr. Bobby Jones, Michael Johnson, Lewis Gibbs, Merdean Gales, the late Al Hobbs, Mr. Malaco, James Moore, and

Donna Creer, without whom my career in the music industry would not be possible.

Thank you to my husband, Dr. Michael L. Mosley, and my six children for being my biggest cheerleaders and greatest support system. I am the woman I am today because of all of you believing in me and praying for me. I love you all dearly!

Introduction

Over the past 20 years I have been a student of business and ministry. My father, Reverend Douglas Wright, was a businessman and devout pastor. Growing up in a household where my father was both gave me a front row seat to learn about business and ministry simultaneously. This allowed me to absorb a love of the two combined because I had the privilege to witness my father achieving success at both.

Being a daddy's girl also assisted me in embracing the two vocations because I spent a lot of time helping my father in his business and in the church. I can remember my siblings and I helping my father with his landscape business during the weekend and the music ministry at the church on Sundays. I drove the riding lawn mower on Friday and Saturdays, and played the drums and piano on Sundays.

I hated working outdoors due to the hot Texas weather but definitely enjoyed the cool comfortable church on Sundays. If my sister was to comment right now she would say, "Annilia, you had it easy because I had to push the lawn mower, not ride it!"

"Well," I would say, "I'm sorry sister! I was the oldest and dad knew if I didn't ride the lawn mower I would have to have too many water breaks and we would be all day trying to finish our workload. Thanks sister for being the harder worker outdoors!"

These working experiences taught me so many lessons in life. For example, I decided early on that I definitely would get an education and work hard to learn whatever I could so I wouldn't have to mow lawns after I left my parents' house. I had a plan that started in the music ministry and then moved on to the music industry.

It started the day my father went and bought an old piano, drums, and a guitar from a pawn shop. He brought them home and called the entire family together. He told us that God had called him to pastor and he wanted his children to assist him in ministry.

My father looked at all four of his children at the time and said, "I am going to anoint all of you and pray that God will bless you to play these instruments." He did just that and we experimented on the instruments day in and day out. I really felt sorry for my mother because she didn't sign up for all of this but she supported my father's decision and she even would bake us cookies during our practice sessions.

After months passed by, both of

my parents realized my siblings and I were gifted, and they decided to invest in piano lessons for me and my sister, Kassilia, and guitar lessons for my brother, Douglas II. My little brother Alfred was too young at the time but he eventually grew up and played drums for the church.

This ritual my father did even carried over to our little brother, Savion Wright, the fifth child in our family. He later learned to play five instruments and was featured on the hit FOX singing competition TV show called, "American Idol." Savion went as far as being one of the top 12 boys in the finals.

We all excelled in playing the

instruments that dad prayed for us to learn. I learned to play the piano, drums, bass guitar, and saxophone. I loved to go to church to play during the services. It was a joy for me every Sunday.

Kassilia was the praise and worship leader. She had a strong soprano voice the congregation loved to hear. She was phenomenal, capturing the audience's attention and ushering us all into worship.

My brother, Douglas, knew he could make that bass talk. He was very nonchalant when he played but he would have the crowd standing when he did his bass solos.

In 1996, my grandmother,

Mary Louise Cooper, was watching the Dr. Bobby Jones gospel channel and saw the channel was soliciting new artists to apply to minister on his national TV show. Those who made the show would have the opportunity to minister at his live taping in Las Vegas, Nevada, at the Rio Grand Hotel.

My grandmother contacted my parents and told them to apply to have Kassilia and me as, "The Wright Sisters," try out for the show. The thought of this actually coming to pass was very exciting and motivating. My parents made sure my grandmother received a videotape of a community talent show we had just won so she could mail it to Dr. Bobby Jones' office.

Weeks passed and we thought maybe we didn't make the show, but on a Tuesday evening the phone rang and on the other end was the voice of Dr. Bobby Jones. Those who know his unique voice know it's him when they hear it. I immediately started to scream and let the entire house know, "Dr. Bobby Jones is on our phone!"

My mother was ecstatic and she grabbed the phone to make sure this was real. I remember my sister saying, "I can't believe it - we are going to Vegas! We will be singing on TV and get to meet Dr. Bobby Jones, too."

16

This was an amazing feeling for our entire family. We celebrated and prepared ourselves for the trip of a lifetime. How many young high school kids can say they actually received a personal call from Dr. Bobby Jones and were invited to sing on his national televised program?

We called and broke the news to my grandmother and she was so excited. She laughed and congratulated us. She said, "Okay, girls. Grandma is going to take you shopping for some new clothes." We went to Vegas in style.

I will never forget that experience. It was an epic opportunity and an opened door God used to help pave the way to where we are today. Thank you, Dr. Bobby Jones, for giving "The Wright Sisters" a chance to do what we love on your national platform.

My sister and I traveled to Las Vegas and out of several groups we were one of three who traveled to minister at Disney World in Florida at the Epcot Center. This was a new epic experience we knew God was navigating to get us in position where we are today. After traveling to Florida and singing before thousands of people, we started seeing ourselves growing from just a local sister duo to a national sister duo.

It's amazing how once you start

experiencing the opportunity to impact the lives of people on a broader scale, the more you are motivated to expand your vision, your goals, and reach to impact more.

After that ministry opportunity, we were tapped by a major gospel label to sign a recording deal. Talk about a larger-than-life experience; we were in awe and anticipating a greater opportunity to get our music heard around the world. This just didn't happen to little country girls from a small community in Jasper, Texas. We were humbled by the opportunity to sign with a major label. My sister and I were still in high school when we flew to the label's location. We had the opportunity to meet all the executives and famous musicians who were in the studio during our visit. The studio's owner happened to be there, too. The A&R rep (artists & repertoire - basically, talent scout) who was hosting us during the day promised us so many wonderful things. He said, "People are going to know you all around the world. You will be able to buy a nice car with the money you're about to make."

Hearing this was music to our teenaged ears, especially since my sister didn't have a car. It was an amazing experience and we were overjoyed. The label's entire team made us feel like rock stars! We just knew we were going to sign and take our music ministry and career to the next dimension.

We were minors at the time, so when it came down to signing the contract, everything had to go through my parents. The label executive had to schedule a separate meeting with them to finalize the deal but there was one problem. My parents knew nothing about the music industry or about music contracts.

Before leaving the city, we had a final meeting with the label's A&R rep. He said that because we wrote all of our music, he would give us a great deal and would take great care of us as artists. He said that for all of the music we wrote he would make sure we got 100% writer's credit and he would get 100% of publishing.

If he had taken the time to investigate whether we were knowledgeable about the music business, he wouldn't have made such a stupid offer. I believe he thought us little country girls who knew nothing about the business side of the industry. Oh, but he was very wrong.

I must give a lot of the credit to Dr. Bobby Jones who made sure we were educated at his Artist Retreats in Las Vegas. Also, I thank God for making me very passionate about learning the business side of the music industry at a young age. Because I was a student of the industry and a steady reader about the music business, I knew how to distinguish between a good deal and a bad deal. I knew early on this wouldn't be the dream record deal we were looking forward to. I knew we would have to do a lot of negotiating or we would not be signing this deal. So I said nothing and acted like I didn't know anything.

I said to myself, "This man thinks we are stupid!" I was so disappointed because being in the gospel industry you would think everyone involved operated with integrity and had the best interests in mind for all people. Well, "The Wright Sisters" learned at an early age that wasn't the case.

After listening to this crooked business label executive, I finally responded respectfully by stating whatever deal we agreed to, it would be my parents who would be in touch to finalize everything. He responded with a smile saying, "I'm going to make you all superstars!"

I said underneath my breath, "Not with 100% of publishing." Then he asked my sister and me if we were ready to sign with the label and I said quickly, "Give us until Monday to pray about it and I will have my father call you to let you know what we've decided."

So we left for Texas on that Saturday and once we got home I immediately shared my concerns with my father. He said, "I will talk with the label executive on Monday."

I already knew if the label executive wasn't going to be fair about the publishing, there was no need for me to pray about the situation. I am one who believes that prayer is always in order but I also believe we don't have to pray about common sense decisions that we know will put us at a disadvantage. For example, there is no need to pray and ask God if can you be successful in life when God has made it clear in his word that he wants you to be the head and not the tail. God says, "But remember the Lord your God, for it is he who gives you the ability to produce wealth." (Deuteronomy 8:18 NIV) God wants us to be "good stewards" over the power he has given us and wants every one of us to live a life of victory, privilege, and success.

When you are in situations like the one my sister and I were in, don't be manipulated by the alluring things people offer and know that you desire, and end up signing over all of your power. Giving all of your power away is not being a good steward over the power God has given to you. Protect your power and be lead by God on how much power to render in the right place and at the right time.

Please, don't get me wrong because I do believe in contracts and agreements. I believe that contracts should benefit both parties, not just one. In your business decisions always make sure you are going into deals and partnerships that are fair and beneficial to you and the other parties involved.

The very next day on Sunday after church, the phone rang and guess who it was?

It was the A&R rep from the label asking to speak with my father. He said he needed to hurry and close

the deal. I said, "Hold on please, sir."
I put the phone down and ran to my
father's bedroom and said, "Dad, he's
on the phone."

My dad said, "Who?"

I said, "The record executive.
He said he needed to close the deal
today."

Dad said, "Okay," so I followed
him back to the living room where I
laid the phone down and he picked it
up quickly and said, "Hello."

The record executive said, "Mr.
Wright, I was really impressed with
your daughters and I'm ready to get
them signed."

My father replied, "Well,
Annilia had an issue with the

publishing you said you would offer."

The executive responded, "I'm giving them 100% writer's credit," and my dad told him to hold on.

Then my dad looked at me and said, "The man said he is giving you all 100% writer's credit."

I said, "Dad, I know we are the ones who wrote the music. That is a given."

Then my dad asked, "What do you want to do, Annilia?"

"Tell him we can do 50% publishing and he can take 50% publishing."

My father relayed the message and the record executive said, "Oh no, we cannot do that under any circumstances. I can't close this deal unless we have 100% publishing."

So I told my dad to tell him it was nice meeting him and the rest of the team and, "unfortunately, we cannot work with those terms. If he cannot offer a fair deal then we have nothing to discuss further."

The record executive said, "I could have made your daughters superstars."

My father replied, "We prayed about it and it's not going to be a good fit for them, so thank you for your call and have a good day, sir."

Please understand we were young and excited but we did not allow our excitement to lock us into a slave contract. I had heard about famous celebrity artists who allowed their excitement of signing with a major label to cause them years of unhealthy sacrifices. Many had worked, toured, and released multiple projects, and didn't have much to show for all the hard work they had done. I'm so glad God allowed us to get educated a few years before to prepare us for the wolves in sheep's clothing. This experience was the beginning of a lifelong passion to educate myself so I could help empower other artists. I wasn't satisfied with just being an artist anymore. I now wanted to establish myself as a music executive so I could be to artists what the crooked label executive wasn't to my sister and me.

This experience taught me to be prepared because if you're not, it can ruin your life and everything you have worked hard to build. This experience became the beginning of a passionate, driven assignment to help people just like you posture yourself for greater success in whatever industry you are in.

The key strategies you will read in this book will help create greater leverage and insight that will allow you to be in a better position to thrive and succeed. I congratulate you now because after reading this book, your life will never be the same - if you apply the strategies to your life.

When you complete this book, I encourage you to share it with those you love and pass it down to those who look up to you. This can be a great read for your leadership team, protégé, and anyone whom you may manage. Enjoy my experiences and life lessons that have accelerated my career and brand to great heights.

Chapter 1
12 Key Ingredients for Accelerated Success

Plato said that the study of number symbolism is one of, "the highest levels of knowledge." The number 12 signifies perfection and represents the completed cycle of life experiences. In the Bible, Jacob had twelve sons and they are considered the ancestors of the Twelve Tribes of Israel.

I believe there is great significance in the number 12. When you think about rehabilitation programs, they use the 12-step program. It is very significant in a particular healing process to succeed in life again.

If we look back in history, you can learn that the number 12 has been used frequently by God[1] and successful leaders in order to establish a solid foundation for success. With this in mind, I would like to share the 12 key ingredients that have produced accelerated success for me within the past few years. I must say I didn't always know how to merge these magical ingredients together or know when to utilize them to create leverage for my success but thanks to

---

[1]

http://www.patheos.com/blogs/christiancrier/2014/09/28/what-does-the-number-twelve-12-mean-or-represent-in-the-bible/

a lot of trial and error, I can finally say that I have established the right combination of ingredients that has produced a level of success for me.

When I think about these successful ingredients, I can't help but reminisce back to my summers in Mississippi with my grandmother, Annie Mae Wright. She was one of the best cooks I've ever met. This woman was the mother of fourteen children and the owner of a farm with my grandfather, Clovis Wright. They raised everything they needed to feed their children, and I think back to when I would see my grandmother in the kitchen preparing cakes, pies, soul food, and her famous sweet tea. She had certain ingredients she used in everything she prepared for us to make that particular dish taste delightful. Grandma would take her time cooking each dish because she knew if she rushed the process, she could possibly forget key ingredients and mess up the dish.

I remember her taking time to teach me how to cook her famous collard greens, and I had finished cleaning the greens and put them in the pot with the ham hocks to cook. I had the fire up too hot and she said, "You want to take your time cooking the greens so the seasoning can have time to get in the greens. If you cook them too fast, the greens will not be

tender and tasty." Then she added,
"Perfection takes time and it will be
worth the wait." I always remembered
those words and learned to allow that
to carry over into every area of my
life.

1st Key

The first key ingredient is
having a "**self-assured purposeful
plan in place**." The Bible says, "write
down the revelation and make it
plain." (Habakkuk 2:2 NIV) Writing
down your vision is necessary before
moving forward to ensure you are
confident in what you want to
accomplish. Having a clear plan in

place helps you and others to see what will become a reality.

2nd Key

The second key ingredient is having a mind to, **"work the plan until it manifests."** In scripture, "Faith without works is dead." (James 2:20 NKJV) You have to work the vision and business God has placed in your heart.

3rd Key

The third key ingredient is, **"surround yourself with significant knowledge"** that will help manifest the plan you have in place. Significant knowledge refers to the specific instructions or the blueprint that will help get you to where you are trying to go. For example, if you are trying to drive to Texas from California, there are specific highways you must take in order to get to your destination. Surround yourself with people and information that will help you get directly to your goals in life.

4th Key

The fourth key ingredient is to, **"connect with a mentor who has a track record of being successful in your industry,"** and glean from their experiences by listening.

5th Key

The fifth key ingredient is to, **"embrace self-discipline and focused thoughts."** He who maintains self-discipline throughout the course of a goal understands the value of purpose. "Focused thoughts" that are aimed to create positive outcomes in the vision will bring about successful results.

6th Key

The sixth key ingredient is to, **"have a measurable and working**

system in place." When you have a measurable system in place, you can gauge the success or failure of a plan. When I think about my first job during my sophomore year in high school, I think about working at McDonalds in Wal-Mart. It was amazing to me the system McDonalds had in place; high schoolers could run it. My manager was a senior in high school at the time and this taught me at an early age that when you have a measurable system in place, you can win BIG.

7th Key

The seventh key ingredient is to

embrace **"balance"** in every area of your life. Make sure you are finding time to live in the now with family and friends. Take time to go to the beach, get a massage, take a walk, vacation with family, or sleep in with your lover. Make sure you are taking time to break away from the work of the vision, so that you can reboot or recharge yourself. This is very healthy for you, your family life, and for the longevity of your vision.

8th Key

The eighth key ingredient is to, **"be flexible."** Sometimes in our efforts to achieve success we can be headstrong about how everything needs to play out, but be open to other options that may still help you get to the goal at hand. There are times you may have to change the direction but it's okay; you just want to complete the goal.

9th Key

The ninth key ingredient is to create the **"Dream Team."** You want to make sure you have like-minded people on your team. Those you chose should have an understanding of what the goal is and be willing to do everything within their power to make it become a reality. The Bible states, "where two or three gather in my name, there am I with them." (Matthew 18:20 NIV) I believe God is saying, "Those who come together in love, understanding, and with a mind to succeed, I will bless their work."

In the case of the people in the biblical story of the "Tower of Babel," God changed the language and what the people set out to accomplish did not happen. Sometimes God will not allow certain things to occur because it just may not meet the bigger plans God already has in store for you. This is why we should find ways to commune with God to make sure we are in synch with what he wants for us.

10th Key

The tenth key ingredient is to, **"market the vision BIG."** You want to create a promotional campaign around the launch of this new innovative vision. It is wise to find ways to make the target audience feel a part of the initiative. Keep in mind that people support vision, especially a vision they can relate to. For example, take Nike's marketing campaign is "Just Do it." This is a statement many can identify with and want to associate themselves with. So ask yourself a question: why would your target audience want to be associated with your vision?

11th Key

The eleventh key ingredient is to, **"be a giver."** The Bible says that it is better to give than to receive. (Acts 20:35 NIV) I believe when you learn you should teach. It is very important that you give back. My parents raised me that way and I have always been a person who reached back and helped those who want to improve in their life. I believe there will come a time in life where you will look back and see what all you have accomplished but it would be nice to have others look back and say, "Because of you, I am a better person."

I believe that as we strive for greater in life, it makes life worth it to be able to share pieces of yourself with others along the way. Don't be selfish; give back and you will be blessed beyond measure.

12th Key

The twelfth key ingredient is to, **"honor God and be grateful."** It is very important that you honor God for the gifts and opportunities to improve the world. You have been chosen to fulfill a great vision that will make life better for those who are privileged to experience the vision. Also learn to be grateful for everything, even the challenges that arise. The Bible states, these trials come to make us stronger. (James 1:2-4 NIV) For every challenge that arises in the process of fulfilling your vision, look at it as an opportunity to be strengthened. The stronger and wiser you become, the more valuable you become to effectively lead others into greatness.

Chapter 2

There is Purpose in Encouraging You!

While I was in prayer, the Lord gave me a word for you! He said that you have purpose and in order to fulfill your purpose, you must not give up or quit.

I was once in a place where I felt like I did not matter anymore. I began to lose hope in all the things God had promised. I began to convince myself that I was finished because the phone calls stopped coming for me to come preach or to sing. I had the audacity to measure my ministry by how many calls I received. Since I was not receiving as many calls as usual I began to question God. I asked him, "Lord, do you still want me to preach? Lord, do you still want me to sing?"

Almost instantaneously God replied, "Yes!" Philippians 1:6 NIV reads, "being confident of this, that he who began a good work in you will carry it on to completion until the day of Christ Jesus." God was saying, "Yes! I want you to continue to go ye therefore and teach all nations baptizing them in the name of the father, son and the Holy Ghost." (Matthew 28:19 KVJ)

Then I said, "Lord, why am I not getting calls anymore? "

The Lord replied, "I need you to focus on home."

I said, "At home, but everything is alright at home and by the way, you called me into full time ministry and this is the way I pay the bills."

God said, "Yes, but don't forget it's me who supplies all of your needs according to my riches in glory. So daughter, don't get confused or sidetracked because if I called you and you are walking in my will, your provisions will be made."

Your Provision is Connected to Your Purpose!

God's rebuttal to my doubt did

not surprise me, but it reignited my spirit. Then the Lord said, "Your provision is always connected to your purpose."

So I responded questioningly, "Lord, as long as I am obedient to you and stay in your will, provisions will be made for me?"

He said, "Yes!" I know that you are thinking of the struggles you are faced with. You've spent all of your money to get to this conference, retreat, or convention and now you're praying that you have enough money to cover all your expenses and then make it home. Well, I believe there comes a time in ministry when you must leap out on faith and give God a chance to create your original miracle; a miracle designed and sculpted just for you and your desperate situation. So for those of you who have chosen to leap out on faith, ignoring fear, blocking out doubt, and eliminating unbelief, count it all joy! This faith walk is the beginning of your testament, of the manifestation that the Lord is truly more than enough.

There is Purpose in Reaching Out!

What do you expect while you are here? Most people are looking for love, acceptance, and encouragement. I pray you meet someone who will be reachable enough to speak a word of encouragement to you. Just like Dr. Bobby Jones and so many others encouraged me when I first came into the music industry over seventeen years ago. These individuals were some of the people God used to speak life into my vision and dreams. I truly thank God for them. Because of their encouragement, their positive words evolved into fuel that sustained and invigorated my determination.

I am committed to and

ceaselessly learning in this industry.
You may not meet the same people I
have, but I speak life into you and
your vision.

Many times we travel looking
for validation from people we don't
even know but God is speaking
through me to let you know: your
ministry is powerful! You are unique
and different, not like anyone else!
You are anointed and wonderful in his
eyes! He applauds you for having the
courage to believe in him enough to
invest in yourself by coming to this
retreat, conference, or convention.
You may not know me and you may
rather hear these words from your
favorite preacher, artist, or TV

56

personality, but God chose me at this time to speak life into you. I pray that I've said something to encourage you to keep on because you are an imperative part of the body of Christ. Because you are so vital to the kingdom, that means God has already placed something special inside of you that authenticates you and makes you unique. You are the only one of you that God created. So be yourself, represent God in excellence, don't quit, and be obedient to what God has placed in your spirit to do.

Learn to accept and understand that seasons will change in ministry! "What do I do when?"

I say to you that I believe the Lord can change the shifts in our ministry or even the assignment just like any "normal" 9 to 5 job. You may not be on the road, but God can give you an assignment right in your own back yard to help your mother, father, sister, brother, husband, wife, children, church, or someone in your community. You may not be traveling across the country ministering abroad, but you are still just as important to God as those who are traveling around the world. Maybe you were traveling cross country singing and preaching but the calls have stopped, and you have become devastated and feel the same way I felt, but be encouraged! Take the time to get in that secret place where God can minister to you because he has directions for you. The Bible says, "Trust in the Lord with all your heart, and lean not on your own understanding; in all your ways acknowledge Him, and He shall direct your paths." (Proverbs 3:5-6 NKJV)

Chapter 3
What Happened to Serving?

Are you ready to serve even if God calls you from the field into the house? I came off the field into the house and I found myself serving, and in that time, God deposited many seeds in my spirit and caused me to birth more fruit to share with various people whom I have come into contact with.

I've realized in the various phases of serving, that God will teach you and prepare you for your next assignment. In many cases, we as leaders sometimes do not want to "go back" to serving, especially when we get comfortable with others serving us. Yes, you can get complacent and accustomed to the pampering of ministries that call on you to minister. They have prepared your favorite fruit tray in your dressing room. You are being picked up in your favorite limo, with your favorite tea and water ready in the cup holders. Yes, I pray that in your flow in ministry that you do not forget others, especially at home.

Serving is not just about getting up and singing your song, preaching your sermon, or giving someone a word over your radio broadcast. Serving is about being available to help someone other than yourself without looking for compensation in return. It's all about being available to help someone else learn about what you do, and for whom you do it. I truly believe that those who embrace their opportunities to serve and serve well, God shall promote in time. I can remember all of the leaders I have served over the years in their ministries and all of them had a great anointing on their lives. I believe because I served these great leaders with humility and great work ethic, God must have seen me and now he has rewarded my life in so many wonderful ways. I thank God I had great mentors to prepare me for the work I do today.

Mentoring Makes You Immortal!

Immortality through mentoring? If you impart some of yourself in others, when you do leave this life, a portion of you remains.

What happened to mentoring? Years ago we didn't have to ask the musician to teach us how to play the piano. If you were found by the piano after service, that next week the pianist would have you sitting next to them, coaching you on how to play during the service. What happened to the choir directors who would teach discipline, dynamics, dress codes, and structure? What happened to the deacons who would train the younger boys to pray? What happened to the people in ministry who didn't mind sharing who they were and what they represented to those who were willing and ready to learn? I believe God wants us all to walk in our purpose but if you're not helping anyone while you are on your journey in this life, you need to reevaluate your life and ministry. God himself sent his son Jesus to give us a pattern and a mentor who would exemplify his unconditional love for us. So if you want to be effective in your ministry, make a decision to try and touch every life that comes into yours because love is one of our most powerful tools. Find a way to help and love those whom you can.

Prayer

I pray for the success of your ministry and for those who will believe enough in you to sow their encouragement, resources, and support. I pray that you will do everything within your power to educate yourself and reach back to help someone else. I pray that you are humble enough to stay planted in a local church so that you can grow and mature beyond your wildest dreams. I pray for all of those who play a part in the production of your life and ministry, that they may maintain good intentions and be a blessing to you. I pray that God will have his way with all of us, that we will lead lives of purpose, integrity, and peace with all mankind. Lastly, I pray that after you read this book, you gain more knowledge, encouragement, determination, and unequivocal expectation in order to move with better precision to obtain greater success. I speak now that you will succeed and be a light of inspiration to the world.

Chapter 4
Finance:
To Thine Own Self Be True

That if we intend to operate from a place of true faith we must operate from a place of true knowledge.

The Bible says, "And you shall know the truth, and the truth shall make you free." (John 8:32 NKJV) I have to be honest with myself in order to grow. There have been times I've done something and then been so angry at myself because I knew better. The pain I felt at the time, ugggghhh! The disappointment I felt sent me into a rage. That moment I had to sever and remember to take time to allow myself to sit in that pain. I owed it to myself to sit in the disappointment so that I would never do what I had done again.

So what did I do? I took all of my money and put it into one investment deal where I did not properly calculate the realistic outcomes of my financial success. In other words, I put all the money I worked hard for over the past few years into something that had no financial guarantee of success. I had to deal with the consequences of not properly planning a successful strategy to regain some of my investment before I spent all the money.

My father taught me as a young girl to never put all of your eggs in one basket. In other words, never put all your resources in one area hoping that it will always be there for you. He said things change, seasons change, so diversify. You will appreciate this if something you depend on leaves or doesn't yield what you are counting on it to deliver.

My father also taught me to create multiple streams of income so you never position yourself to rely on a single source of income. I wish I had that wisdom in that particular season of my life regarding how to properly manage and juggle the many responsibilities I had on my plate.

In keeping up multiple streams of income, it definitely takes putting priorities in place and executing them daily. It also takes discipline to ensure your life is organized to accomplish this task. I had found myself spending more time trying to build up a particular business. I started to let go of building up the other streams of income I had in place. The excitement of making business B a success was more exciting for me at the time, so I lost half of the income coming in from business A. I was taking hours that I normally worked in business A and used those hours to build up business B. I was literally putting in over 90 hours a week into business B and it wasn't yielding me even 25% back of what I had put into the business.

After months has passed, I looked in the business account and there it was, a snapshot of the reality I was in and that was almost broke. I still needed to make this investment work but now I had lost a great amount of the income I was making and I was here still trying to figure out how not to lose my investment with business B.

In looking at the lack of financial income to continue business B, I literally got up and ran outside and started talking to God. I stood outside for at least an hour staring into the sky feeling lost and alone because I leaped out on faith to do this and now I didn't have the financial support to continue. I was so angry with myself because I know business, but I waited too long to do an environmental scan on my business to make sure I put things in place to protect it. I wanted to be angry with God but at the same time, I had to take full responsibility for myself and the decision I had made that didn't position the business to yield money back within three to six months. If I just would have created a more comprehensive plan in raising funds on a regular basis, I could have been in a better financial position. If I would have raised at least 40% of the funds needed to properly create a safety net for the business, I wouldn't be in this place. If I would have just paced myself and not rushed into it, I could have saved myself from this feeling of failure.

I have now learned that sometimes you have to sit with bad decisions you have made and really mentally identify where you went wrong. Because when you take time to identify what went wrong, then that becomes a lesson learned.

There are many people who call my experience failure but I call it a lesson learned. There are simple lessons you can learn in life on your journey and there are expensive ones. For some these are crucial and life-altering lessons. This is why it's so important that we surround ourselves with mentors. You must learn to connect with mentors who have walked the path that you desire to walk. Learn to identify mentors who have the skill sets and experience you don't and it will help you miss many of the pitfalls and the ditches others have fallen into.

During this particular stage of my life, I had to come to grips with myself and call my actions of irresponsibility out to the forefront. I had to be real and honest with myself, especially if I was going to experience better ahead. I had to live with the fact I had been operating under the notion that I had hoped this business would work out instead of putting a calculated plan in place to give me some guaranteed success.

There are a lot of people who have done what I have done and if they are honest, it doesn't feel good to put in a lot of work only to get nothing in return. Who wants to work for free especially when you have bills to pay? I know of some artists, musicians, and business professionals who have made these same mistakes of proceeding forward based on their faith and passion. In any industry you choose to operate in and invest your money, there is always going to be some reasonable doubt that you will see immediate success. In those cases we have to educate ourselves, and stop spinning our wheels and just doing things because it feels good to us. We have to do things in an intellectual way. We must do our homework first! The Bible tells us, "Study to show thyself approved unto God." (2 Timothy 2:15 KJ21) We must do this in every area of our lives or we will continue to find ourselves working from a place of passion and receiving for our effort a disappointing return.

What are some tools we can use to help us go beyond our faith and passion to better prepare for success?

Learn to create a SWOT analysis in your business/ministry. A SWOT analysis is a study tool you can use to identify your organization's internal Strengths and Weaknesses, as well as its external Opportunities and Threats (SWOT). This is what I now use to manage my vision and create better ways to guarantee greater success in my businesses and ministry. (For those interested in learning more about exactly how SWOT works, Mind Tools is a great resource.)

Also, when I have all of my

goals in place, my team and I work to achieve benchmarks we have set and then we run a monthly environmental scan to make sure we are on target and creating financial growth for my businesses. An environmental scan is a process that systematically surveys and interprets relevant data to identify external opportunities and threats. If you are in ministry or business, this is a process that needs to be incorporated on a regular basis. There is not a successful ministry or business in operation that does not embrace this opportunity. This process also allows you to gather information about the external world, competitors, and the demand for what your company/ministry has to offer.

My friend, we can still walk in faith while educating ourselves on how to become better stewards over what God has given us. I know the scripture says, "we walk by faith and not by sight" (2 Corinthians 5:7 NKJV) but God never intended for us to walk in ignorance. If faith without works is dead, then we have a responsibility to work effectively. In order for us to work effectively in ministry and business, we must educate ourselves and surround ourselves with truth that will make us free.

So I say this with love: if we

intend to operate from a place of true faith, we must operate from a place of true knowledge of where we are and where we're trying to get to. If you are tired of finding yourself back in the same place after a period of time, either you're not educating yourself properly, or you haven't learned to apply the knowledge that you have learned. In order for us to grow and progress, we have to learn to apply the necessary knowledge that will get us to the place we desire.

It is time for us to stop lying to ourselves, doing things that will continue to imprison us within the places we are trying to escape. For example, I am trying to be wiser in my financial decisions and position myself to be better. Also, I want to be able to do more to help others, but first I have to help myself. So my first steps are to get one of my businesses financially stable, and then focus on the next and before I know it, they both will be thriving.

I can then position myself to become more financially healthy and stable in order to mentor more people to do the same in business and ministry. While I am becoming better, I must never forget what past actions took me down the wrong path, and make sure I don't do the same things again to set my progress backwards. Therefore, if you really want better, if you want to experience better, if you want to do better, then you have to become better first!

The Bible says we must not be among those, "having a form of godliness but denying its power," (2 Timothy 3:5 NIV) because when we operate from a fake place, we cheat ourselves out of experiencing a life of true fulfillment. You can have a form of prosperity and deny the power thereof by having prosperous material things but a poverty mindset. You can live in the biggest house, drive an expensive car, wear the latest designer clothing, but have no money in the bank, trying to keep up with the Joneses. Is that really success? I believe true success is when you can live a comfortable life and not ever be worried about if you're going to be able to pay your bills every month. This is why it is important for us to live within our means and not above them.

One of my mentors, a self made millionaire, taught me their success formula for creating financial stability. When you have an increase, pay your 10% immediately to God. In the Church we call that our tithes. Next, pay yourself by taking 25% and putting it in an investment portfolio that will go towards long term investing. This is money you do not touch but invest and when you retire, instead of depending on a 401K from a job, you can create your own safety net with years of compound interest.

Then take 45% and pay your bills before they are due or at the very least, on time. Take the remaining 20% and save it for cash flow and to have fun. Lastly, my mentor stated that everyone will not be willing to make these sacrifices but for those who are ready, that's when their teacher will appear. So I hope today you're ready to move into greater financial stability.

My friend, knowledge isn't power unless you know how to effectively apply the knowledge you've learned. Again, this is why the most valuable investment you can ever give yourself is a great mentor. It is so important to understand that having the wealth of the knowledge of how to be debt-free is one thing but actually being debt-free is another. I believe having a plethora of material things doesn't make you a prosperous person. What makes you a prosperous person is when you can work hard and achieve success, and then find ways to give back to others. You have many people who have the ability to acquire the material things, but in many cases do not have the wherewithal and the knowledge on how to maintain it. This is why it is important for us to educate ourselves and apply that knowledge; so we can become true living expressions of what it means to be prosperous and wealthy.

When you get sick and tired of ending up in the same place in life, you will do the work. For example, when the children of Israel walked around the wilderness for 40 long years without seeing much progress in their lives, I can't imagine how frustrated they were. If you are ready for success in your finances, you will take steps to become better at managing them. Albert Einstein stated that doing the same thing over and over again and expecting different results is the definition of insanity.

When you get tired of your situation, you will make a conscious decision to do something different. Then and only then will that be a sign that you truly get it! If you want to become better in your finances, you're going to have to make a conscious decision to educate yourself and apply the necessary actions required to become financially independent.

On this day, a few years ago, I made a decision that would be the last day I would have to call a friend or family member and ask them to transfer money into my account so I could pay my bills. Even though I was single during this time and had my father's support, it still felt humiliating to go back and ask for help. This feeling of failure, the feeling of disappointment, the feeling of hopelessness, the feeling of letting myself down put me in a bad space. I even questioned my faith at times and wondered what was it that I was missing. I had been walking in ignorance for too long and it was time for a change. The Bible declares, "For everyone to whom much is given, from him much will be required." (Luke 12:48 NKJV) The more knowledge you get, the more you are required to be a good steward over it. After understanding this crucial element of success, then it is our responsibility to apply the necessary knowledge in the areas we hope to succeed in so that our life and ministry/ business can become better.

For example, look at those who love to invest money before investors become partners with others. They create safety nets around their deals, so that if things do not go well, they are still protected. This is being a good steward over your finances, your time, your resources, and your influence.

Having said that, don't do business with people without a contract. I have learned people may change their minds and sometimes you may even change your mind once you discover you're doing business with a person who does not share your ethical practices.

I honestly believe God gives great blessings to those who believe and who are good stewards over their current blessings. In the Bible, there is a parable that really brings this concept to life. It's called the "Parable of the Talents." I want to focus on verses 19-29 in Matthew 25 (ESV).

19 Now after a long time the master of those servants came and settled accounts with them. 20 And he who had received the five talents came forward, bringing five talents more, saying, 'Master, you delivered to me five talents; here I have made five talents more.' *21 His master said to him, 'Well done, good and faithful servant. You have been faithful over a little; I will set you over much. Enter into the joy of your master.' 22 And he also who had the two talents came forward, saying, 'Master, you delivered to me two talents; here I have made two talents more.' 23 His master said to him, 'Well done, good and faithful servant. You have been faithful over a little; I will set you over much. Enter into the joy of your master.' 24 He also who had received the one talent came forward, saying, 'Master, I knew you to be a hard man, reaping where you did not sow, and gathering where you scattered no* *seed, ²⁵ so I was afraid, and I went and hid your talent in the ground. Here you have what is yours.' ²⁶ But his master answered him, 'You wicked and slothful servant! You knew that I reap where I have not sown and gather where I scattered no seed? ²⁷ Then you ought to have invested my money with the bankers, and at my coming I should have received what was my own with interest. ²⁸ So take the talent from him and give it to him who has the ten talents. ²⁹ For to everyone who has will more be given, and he will have an abundance. But from the one who has not, even what he has will be taken away.*

The text shows that even God expects us to multiply what he entrusts in our hands. So ask yourself a question, "Can God count on me to multiple what he has put in my hands to oversee?" Think for a moment, "Are you one who every time you get money, you spend it immediately?" Do you find yourself using the finances God has entrusted you with on things that will not bring you back a return or yield you into a better financial position? These are hard questions to ask yourself if you have struggled in the area of your finances for some time. Allow this book to encourage you and mentor you to a better mentality about your stewardship. I can assure you that if you take time and do the work, you will become better at mastering your finances.

If you want to become free, you need to become S.O.L.I.D. in your financial freedom journey. This is my acronym to encourage you to become SOLID in your Financial Freedom Mindset:

S = sick
O= of
L= losing
I = in
D=developmental

Financial Freedom

When you get sick of losing, you find a way to get motivated to win!

Hopefully this message can encourage you and soften your heart, and motivate you to take a look and evaluate your life. Please know God loves you and is counting on you to grow and improve.

My question to you today is, "Are you using your gifts to bring greater value to the kingdom of God?" Evaluate your station in life, evaluate your influences, evaluate your talents, evaluate your skills, evaluate your maximum potential. When we take time to be a good steward, I believe

God sees us and he will reward us with even more when he sees that he can trust us.

I pray as you read this you begin to think of someone else that you care about and who can benefit from this chapter. Be empowered and become better today in your finances! This is your hour to prepare because where God is taking you, it will benefit you now to start your journey of mastering this important element in your ministry/business.

Chapter 5
"Create a Proven Ritual System"

If you want to make a difference in ministry, the music industry, business, or in someone's life, you must create an extraordinary ritual system that will condition you to be at your best mentally, spiritually, physically, and emotionally. Learning to embrace this is only the beginning of what it takes to establish yourself as a solid and healthy contributor/leading trailblazer in your industry. Taking time to carefully mature in every area of your life creates greater leverage for you in the long run. It also creates longevity for you in your industry.

Those who have gracefully traveled through their journey and process in business and ministry have seen days of challenges and success. Those who have arrived and excelled have been matured in areas that others have not. This is why the four crucial elements of success - mental, spiritual, physical, emotional - are important for you to know and understand. When you really get the understanding and purpose of going through a process, you will learn to become appreciative of the challenges you face along your journey to success. I will be sharing a piece of my foundational journey of success and I know you can gain some great nuggets of truth to help you on your own journey to greater success.

The Bible tells us that we can do all things through Christ that strengthens us. (Philippians 4:13) I believe this passage and I have lived in this passage for years. I truly stand by this text and teach it to my children. I believe sometimes people operate from a place of defeat, doubt, second-guessing themselves, and sometimes don't really understand how to use this text to their advantage.

In order for us to be able to do all things through Christ, we must understand the true meaning of what the writer was trying to interpret for us. When we look at the Greek meaning of *"The Christ,"* it is *"Christos,"* which also means *"anointed."* In the religious community I come from, it was taught that the anointing signifies, "one that is chosen by God and is set apart to do a great work." I believe that we are all capable of doing a great work for a greater cause, call, and purpose. This leads me to a very important lesson I learned as a little girl from my father.

My father, pastor Douglas Wright, taught me, "If you want to do extraordinary things in life, you must BECOME extraordinary."

My father taught me this through discipline. He was the disciplinarian in our family and he did not play. He was a man raised during the Civil Rights movement in the small town of Hickory, Mississippi, born to my grandfather, Rev. Clovis Victor Wright, who was a United Methodist Pastor and farmer, and my grandmother, who was a seamstress and share cropper. My father was one of 14 children raised by my grandparents on their farm. Yes, they were very poor when it came to material things but my father's life experience yielded the wealth of an extraordinary work ethic and high moral standards.

My father worked very hard to pass down the work ethic he learned on the farm in Mississippi to his young children. My father was a professional runner and he ran long distance 3K's and 5K's throughout the states and competed on a high level for years. He started training my siblings and me to run long distance at the early age of seven, and it was a consistent effort on his part and our part. In our household, my father required us to run one mile a day up to our middle school years and then he increased it to two miles during our high school years.

We didn't always run on the weekends because we had more work cut out for us at his landscape business. On Saturdays, we pushed lawnmowers, raked leaves, and picked up sticks and trash. We worked hard during the winter and in the torturous Texas summer heat. I can remember us mowing 23 yards in one day and boy, we were exhausted.

On Sundays, we went to church because my father was a pastor of three churches in the United Methodist Church.

From an early age, my father worked to condition us to be active participants in our own personal lives through discipline. He always would say, "You don't appreciate me now but when you get older, you're going

103

to love me for what I am teaching you." Well dad, you were right! I do appreciate everything you taught me because it has contributed to a lot of my success in life.

As a child, I could not understand what my father was doing but I now do. He was helping me to develop proven ritual system builders. My dad gifted me with some of his proven ritual system building activities my grandparents passed down to him. He added his own rituals based on the vision God showed him for us as his children.

Through my father's teachings I developed my own set of ritual system builders that I currently pass down to my own children. My ritual system builder is called, "4 Crucial Elements To Success," or, "4CE2Success," for short. These elements are your mental, emotional, spiritual and physical aspects and must be developed on a daily basis. When they are developed properly, you will find you can operate at your highest potential and that there is nothing you cannot achieve in life.

My father helped to develop these elements on a daily basis through the ritual system builder he created for us through running, mowing lawns, and participating in church.

The running developed our

bodies physically and also mentally. My father didn't just tell us to run, he taught us breathing techniques, proper running form, and strategy on how to improve our mile each day. He taught us not to compete with each other as siblings but to compete with ourselves. He timed us every single day and encouraged us to try to beat our time from the day before. He also would run with us, and during our run he would coach us on how to pace ourselves. He knew you could not sprint a mile but you would have to pace yourself. This taught us to pace ourselves in life because life isn't a sprint but it is a marathon. As he coached us to the finish line each day, he would also sometimes race us to push us harder through the finish line.

When we would get near the last stretch, he would cheer and celebrate with us and say, "Finish strong!" Then after we finished he would tell us to keep walking, allow the body to readjust, and then stretch to avoid experiencing cramps later.

This ritual builder taught us to think through things, strategize, pace yourself in life, work smart and not hard, finish strong, compete with yourself and not others, be committed, and take time to breathe, re-acclimate yourself, and celebrate yourself after accomplishing a goal.

When it came to building up my spiritual and emotional areas in life, my mother was a master. My mother, Rosalind Wright, was a homemaker and she literally lived her life centered around my dad, siblings, and me. My mother was always loving and kind. She really gave everything to make us all feel loved, appreciated, and valued.

I remember how my mother took in so many other children in our community and raised them as her own. I am not exaggerating; my mother has helped raised over 60 children through connections at our church and the foster care system. God made her a mother goose. I have great respect for my mother because she loved hard but at the same time, she always told us that when she had my siblings and me, she gave us all back to the LORD. She said she will always love us but no one can out-love God the creator, and I will always remember that.

My mother taught all of us how to pray and develop a personal relationship with God. She would take time to pray with me as a child and even in my adult years she still prays with me. Prayer has been a foundation that has helped bring me peace in my emotions and spiritual journey. With prayer, mother taught me a great ritual builder to help me in my life of success.

In summarizing what the four elements of success are, they are making sure you develop and maintain your mental, spiritual, physical, and emotional state of being. When you achieve this, you have already increased your success in life toward becoming an extraordinary person, which will in return yield you the opportunity to do extraordinary things.

Annilia Wright-Mosley
Biography

Lady Annilia Mosley is a powerful motivational speaker, businesswoman, professor, recording artist, and author. Her rich method of captivating her audience through speaking and singing has caused her to be greatly sought after over the past 15 years. She is the eldest of five children born to Pastor Douglas and Rosalind Wright.

Born with wonderful talent, Lady Annilia has been a prominent speaker, businesswoman, and psalmist for over 15 years. She has toured within the 50 states, Canada, and Paris, France. She is respected for her speaking abilities and has been invited to speak on panels in various arenas including churches, universities, business workshops, and national conventions.

Annilia is a smooth, yet powerful vocalist. The clarity of her tone and powerful delivery has allowed her to be positioned to share the stage with many great national artist such as Mary Mary, Yalonda Adams, Tonex, Trin-i-tee 5:7, Dr.

Bobby Jones, Deitrick Haddon, and Michelle Williams to name a few.

Hardly a novice to the music industry or ministry work, Annilia realized her anointing at an early age. By her teenage years, she had already begun speaking and singing, and went on to start a group with her younger sister called, "The Wright Sisters."

In a true entrepreneurial spirit, Annilia started her record label, W'Righteous Records, and produced the group's first album at the age of 18. This independent album sold over 10,000 copies in several states through a take- it-to-the-street

113

approach. On several occasions, she has appeared on Dr. Bobby Jones Gospel, TBN, Day Star, and in publications such as Gospel Truth, Gospel City, Gospel Flava, and Behind the Scenes Gospel.

Despite the push to immediately further her career as a music artist, Annilia remained sensitive to the spirit and began her now acclaimed work as a music industry insider. Her experiences run the gamut from record executive and stage managing to artist management and production. Her highly praised work attracted the attention of gospel recording artist Kim Burrell who petitioned Annilia to serve as her Executive Assistant and road manager for three years.

After serving, Lady Annilia decided to continue to move forward in her ministry encouraging all through her latest compact disc, "Moving on by Faith!"

Then through divine instruction, Annilia decided to sign three new artists to her label, promoting Johnny Johnson, Trina "Sister Cantaloupe" Jeffrie, and

Russell White to greater success in their careers.

Currently, Annilia resides in Riverside, California, and is working on her second master's degree in Theology at the Claremont School of Theology. She is also a Certified Candidate to become an Elder in the United Methodist Church.

Annilia is founder of the Alfred Wright Education & Justice Foundation and also "The G.I.F.T. E.D. Project," which stands for Growing In Faith Today Equipped & Determined. The goals of these nonprofit organizations are to consistently give back to our youth by promoting higher education, motivation, and success in business.

Giving back to people is one of Annilia's passions. She also presently serves with her husband, Dr. Michael L. Mosley, at his ministry Center of Truth in Houston, Texas, and the "The Success Center" in Riverside, California.

In addition to being a wife, mother, artist, author, motivational speaker, Adjunct Business Professor at Devry University, Lady Annilia

oversees her record label,
W'Righteous Records, and consulting
firm, A.W. Horizons, in the greater
Los Angeles area. She assists business
professionals, ministries, and artists in
branding and ministry development.

      Last but not least,
Annilia's favorite scripture is Romans
8:28, "And we know all things are
working together for the good of them
that love the LORD and that are
called according to his purpose."

For Booking
Annilia Wright-Mosley

Contact our office at
W'Righteous Records / AW Horizons
3410 La Sierra Ave. Ste. F #309
Riverside, CA 92503
909-358-5249
Ladyannilia@wrighteousrecords.com

Copyright © 2017
by Annilia Wright-Mosley

119